EFFECTIVE LEADERSHIP

The essentials

GREGORY ERHABOR

EFFECTIVE LEADERSHIP - THE ESSENTIALS

ISBN: 978-978-790-817-4

Unless otherwise indicated, all scripture quotations are, with kind permission, from the King James Version (KJV), New King James Version (NKJV).

DISCLAIMER
Concerted efforts have been made to acknowledge the author of any quotation inserted in this book. However, there may be a few omissions; especially if the authors are not known or the quotation has become part of common proverbs. The publisher however regrets any of such omissions.

PUBLISHER
Spokesman Communication Ministries
www.spokesmancom.org
gregerhabor7@yahoo.com

DESIGNS & PRINTING
Signet Academic Publishers Ltd.
(Signet Impressions & Designs Ltd.)
joshuawealth77@gmail.com; signetng@gmail.com
www.signet.com.ng. +234 (0) 8034251438

THANKS

I am immensely grateful for the grace of God that has come to my life through the Lord Jesus Christ. It has flooded my heart with love from the Almighty God and tender loving Father of all spirits. I appreciate my daily walk and fellowship with the Blessed Spirit who has inspired me every day. The inspiration for my writings and speeches has always come from the Blessed Spirit and daily meditation on the scriptures.

I also want to appreciate numerous authors through the ages whose works and writings have influenced my thinking and shaped my life.

I am thankful for the numerous opportunities I have had to speak in local churches, assemblies, leadership fora and other platforms. These have immensely helped to shape my thought process and philosophy of life .

I am very grateful to the team of mentors and mentees from all over the world who have inspired my writing and taught me in various ways.

In writing this book, I would like to thank Dr Bimbo Usoroh (nee Akinpelu), who worked with me assiduously. I am very grateful to Dr Kemi Taiwo, Dr Tope Kehinde and Dr Nike Arawomo who worked painstakingly on the editorial aspect of this book and to ensure its successful completion.

I appreciate the invaluable support of my dear wife, Rev Ayodele Erhabor and my wonderful children for their unflinching support and consistent prayers without which I would not have been able to fulfill my diverse roles and assignments.

Above all, I am thankful to God for the opportunity He has given me to lead and serve His people all over the world.

CONTENTS

PREFACE

For many years, I have held numerous academic leadership positions and I have pastored a local church for well over two decades. Although I am still learning, I have acquired a wealth of experience in leadership. This book was inspired by a talk I gave in a Church in York, United Kingdom and it deals with essential principles that govern effective leadership as well as the pitfalls leaders encounter on their journey.

One big thing about leadership is that leaders are essentially those who impact others; they are always "others-driven" rather "than self-centred". Christian leaders have a great responsibility in that Jesus did not only teach about leadership but He modeled leadership as it should be. In Matthew 20:27-28 He said, *"And whosoever will be chief among you, let him be your servant: Just as the Son of Man did not come to be served but to serve and to give His life a ransom for many."* Jesus has become a model not just for Christians but for all leaders.

All over the world, there is a dire need for leaders; nations are collapsing, standards are falling, true leaders are rare and there is a cry for great and effective leaders.

Leadership is like an inverted pyramid and the joy of leadership is that one is able to influence people, institutions and build the upcoming generation. I hope this book will inspire current and future leaders to think of how they can effectively influence and create an atmosphere of change in their generation.

WHO IS AN EFFECTIVE LEADER?

The word "Leader" is derived from the Norse term 'Loder' which literarily means the one person on a Viking raiding ship who knew how to read the lodestone with a crude compass. This means a leader is someone who moves people from one place to the other or from one level to another.

Effectiveness as defined by Peter Drucker in his book, 'The Effective Executive', is **choosing and getting the right things done.** Effectiveness should not be confused with efficiency, which simply means getting things done. Therefore, being an effective leader is not just about getting things done but about getting the right things done.

A leader is the one in charge, the person who convinces others to follow. A great leader inspires confidence in other people and moves them to action.

Leadership is influence and there is a spirit of leadership. It is not a position, a status, not about intelligence quotient or curriculum vitae; it is service, changing the paradigm and making significant positive impact in an institution or a group of people. Harry D. Strunk, the founder of the McCook Daily Gazette and a great humanitarian, once said, ***"service is the rent we pay for the space we occupy in this world".*** Albert Schweitzer, a tireless humanitarian, theologian and Nobel peace prize winner, also said, ***"those who will be happy among you are those who will have sought and found how to serve."*** Leadership is not individual greatness but institutional greatness.

Christ is our biggest model for leadership as He said in Luke 22:27, *"For who is greater, he who sits at the table, or he who serves? Is it not he who sits at the table? Yet I am among you as One who serves."*

Contrary to the general mindset, leadership is not just about positions, it is about:

- **Relationships**

A leader must have a relationship with the people one leads in order to influence them to move forward. As Leonard Sweet, an American theologian, once said ***"The essence of leadership is relationship; influencing people to achieve things together that can't be achieved alone".***

- **Responsibility**

Responsibility has been once defined as "response ability". The great Winston Churchill, an inspirational statesman and valiant soldier in Britain, wrote, ***"The price of greatness is responsibility".***

- **Results**

Effective leadership is not just about making speeches or being liked but about getting results. One of the cardinal ways of knowing a great leader is producing results that will benefit not just the individual but the institution. Result is everything. Peter F. Drucker the great management expert said ***"Leadership is defined by results not attributes".***

- **Recalibrating institutions**

Leaders always ask the "Why not?" question. Bernard Shaw, the Irish playwright said, ***"Some men see things as they are,***

and say, "why?" I dream things as they never were, and say, "why not?"

Great leaders strive to see how they can recalibrate the institution, respond to change and create a pathway for growth. They are not there to complain or explain, they are rather there to reposition the institution for greatness.

> *"Leadership is about making others better as a result of your presence but making sure that impact lasts in your absence" – Harvard Business School.*

Leadership is a great opportunity which comes with all manner of challenges and you do not need to have a title or position before you can be a leader; everyone has the potential to be a leader.

* * * *

THE LEADERSHIP STYLE OF JESUS

Daniel Goleman in his book, "Primal Leadership: Unleashing the Power of Emotional Intelligence" identified different styles of leadership which are coaching, coercive, authoritative, pace-setting, democratic and affiliative. He further explained that these different styles of leadership can be used at different times to get positive results. Robert

Greenfield also talked about the power of servant leadership in his book which has been adopted in many leadership literatures. However, in my own opinion, no one has demonstrated great leadership more than Jesus Christ. He modelled leadership by being the example. He was driven by a mission beyond Himself, He measured His success not in a competitive way but followed the vision He had received from the Father and His influence continues to reverberate through all the ages.

PART ONE

CHARACTERISTICS OF EFFECTIVE LEADERS

one

EFFECTIVE LEADERS HAVE A VISION

A vision is the preferred future, the horizon, the end point, the big picture, the finishing line and it reveals what the world would be like after you might have accomplished your task.

One of the greatest components of leadership is vision. You must first envisage a vision for your life before building a vision for others to follow.

A vision is not just something we can see but something we desire to achieve. Jesus said in John 4:35, *"Do you not say, 'There are still four months and then comes the harvest'? Behold, I say to you, lift up your eyes and look at the fields, for they are already white for harvest."*

A leader must have a long-haul-view. Steven Covey said in his book on '7 Habits of Highly Effective People', to keep the end in view as you start your day and that if you do not make a conscious effort to visualize what you want in life, you will invariably empower people and circumstances to shape your life by default.

Without a vision, the leader is nonexistent. A leader must be able to see, not just with the physical eyes but with the mind's eyes as Hellen Keller, the disability rights activist said, ***"The most pathetic person in the world is someone who has sight but has no vision".***

The Bible further says in Proverbs 29:18 that, *"Where there is no vision, the people perish."* Another version of this verse says, *"Without a vision, the people lose restraint"* (NABRE).

Leaders are people who cultivate a vision for life and lead others to a particular destination. They are important catalysts to driving a vision. In a sense, it is not so much where the bus is going but who is driving the bus.

Jim Collins' level 5 leadership concept developed in his book, 'Good to Great', focuses not only on the vision but on the visioneer. The leader cannot be separate from the vision; the vision is integrated into the leader as the leader is integrated into the vision. When you become a leader, you must first define your vision, think about what you aim to accomplish and what you want the world to be like at the end of your task.

No one can be a true leader if they do not have a plan or a sense of direction for the institution they are leading.

Thomas Carlyle, the great historian and philosopher said, ***"The man without a purpose is like a ship without a rudder, a waif, a nothing, a no man."*** *"If you don't know where you're going, any road will take you there"* Lewis Carroll (An English Author).

The great American civil rights leader, Martin Luther King Jr., talked about vision when he made one of the most iconic speeches in American history at one of the defining moments of the civil rights movement, calling for equality and freedom starting with ***"I have a dream"***.

The vision must be clear, concise, consuming, challenging, compelling; have context and attract commitment. It is also important to write down the vision and share with the people you lead as this helps them know and remember what the institution is all about. Habakkuk 2:2-3 says, *"Then the LORD answered me and said, "Write the vision and make it plain on tablets, that he may run who reads it. For the vision is yet for an appointed time; But at the end it will speak, and it will not lie. Though it tarries, wait for it; Because it will surely come, It will not tarry."*

A quote by Paul Horey, an engineering specialist, puts it quite explicitly, ***"A blind man's world is bounded by the limits of his touch, an ignorant man's world by the limits of his knowledge, a great man's world by the limits of his vision".***

Effective leaders should not only have a vision but they must also have a mission and set goals, which could be short-term and long-term. They must also have a road map with clear strategies, which can be constantly reviewed to achieve their set goals.

Some great institutions have keyed into this principle of having and writing their mission statements which they run by. For instance:

- **Johns Hopkins -** *"That Johns Hopkins hospital will be the world's pre-eminent health care institution and leader in medical education, discovery and innovation".*
- **McDonald's -** *"To be the world's best quick-service restaurant experience".*
- **Microsoft -** *"To empower people through software-anytime, any place and on any device".*

- **Bill Gates –** *"A computer on every desk, in every home running Microsoft software".*
- **Thomas Bata Sr** (founder of Bata International) - *"I was put on the face of the earth to shoe mankind."*
- **Jesus Christ –** *"For I came down from heaven, not to do mine own will, but the will of him that sent me"* (John 6:38).
- **King David –** *"I will behave myself wisely in a perfect way. O when wilt thou come unto me? I will walk within my house with a perfect heart. I will set no wicked thing before mine eyes: I hate the work of them that turn aside; it shall not cleave to me."* (Psalm 101:2-3).
- **Apostle Paul –** *"That I should be the minister of Jesus Christ to the Gentiles, ministering the gospel of God, that the offering up of the Gentiles might be acceptable, being sanctified by the Holy Ghost"* (Romans 15:16).

If you desire to be a great and visionary leader, you must keep dreaming, as Christian Bovee, a New York City writer wrote, ***"One who is contented with what he has done, will never be famous for what he will do".***

two

EFFECTIVE LEADERS LEAD THEMSELVES (SELF-LEADERSHIP)

"Self-leadership is the practice of intentionally influencing your thinking, feeling and actions towards your objectives" (Bryant and Kazan, 2012).

Leadership is intentional; it is emptying oneself into the institution. You cannot lead others when you cannot lead yourself. As a matter of fact, great leadership starts from being able to rule over oneself, master one's emotions, keep boundaries and avoid falling victim of promiscuity or prodigality. Effective leaders should create a balance between successfully delivering the mission and at the same time being aware of the human elements that they have to deal with. They must also avoid being driven by the success syndrome (i.e. success at all cost) that they forget the human element of leadership.

The wise Solomon said *"He that is slow to anger is better than the mighty; and he that ruleth his spirit than he that taketh a city"* (Proverbs 16:32). Apostle Paul said in 2 Corinthians 9:27, *"But I discipline my body and bring it into subjection, lest, when I have preached to others, I myself should become disqualified."*

Great leadership entails having values – principles and standards of behaviour that are desirable. Effective leaders are value-driven and altruistic. The principles leaders live by will ultimately determine their behaviour. Therefore, leaders who desire to exhibit desirable behaviours must develop the 'north principles' described by Steven Covey in his book, 'First things First', which include integrity, moderation, self-discipline, loyalty, responsibility, honesty and patience.

The act of self-leadership is based on what is inside of you as one can give what one does not have. Suddenly becoming a leader does not make one develop leadership traits; one must build a capability before one can build a capacity. When people who are self-centered or egoistic become leaders, it doesn't stop them from being who they are. In fact, leadership exposes a person's true character as Jesus said in Matthew 15:11, *"what goes into a man's mouth does not make him unclean but what comes out of his mouth, that is what makes him unclean."*

Henry S. Truman, the 33rd American president said; *"In reading the lives of great men, I found that the first victory they won was over themselves... **Self-discipline with all of them came first.**"* Self-disciplined leaders are of good character and they prioritize integrity.

According to Dwight D. Eisenhower, the 34th American president; *"**The supreme quality for leadership is unquestionably integrity**. Without it, no real success is possible, whether it is on a section gang, a football field, in an army, or in an office."*

It was said of David in the Bible that, *"So he shepherded them according to the integrity of his heart, and guided them with his skillful hands"* (Psalm 78:72).

Andrea Goodridge, a leadership coach, described four main pillars of self-leadership as follows:

i. **Self-discovery:** identify your values.

ii. **Self-acceptance and personal responsibility:** taking responsibility for one's actions.

iii. **Self-management and personal accountability:** managing one's time and resources effectively.

iv. **Self-growth:** striving to improve oneself and learning to embrace failure as a learning opportunity.

The Bible describes some attributes of a model leader in 1 Timothy 3:2 which says, *"Therefore an overseer must be above reproach, the husband of one wife, sober-minded, self-controlled, respectable, hospitable, able to teach".* 1 Timothy 3:5 further says, *"For if a man does not know how to rule his own house, how will he take care of the church of God?"*

'Taking heed unto yourself' is a prime requirement of leadership. Apostle Paul said in Acts 20:28 *"Take heed therefore unto yourselves, and to all the flock, over the which the Holy Ghost hath made you overseers, to feed the church of God, which he hath purchased with his own blood."*

Being self-conscious of the fact that you are essentially the one others are looking up to is one of the hallmarks of leadership. You set the standard for others, for without a leader's example, the institution crumbles.

Leadership does not start with the flock, the nation or the institution, it starts with you. So, don't wait to see a change in the people you lead, be the change you expect to see in them.

Steve Buchholz, a notable author wrote, ***"A superior leader demonstrates; a great leader inspires."***

three

EFFECTIVE LEADERS ARE RESILIENT

According to the American Psychological Association, resilience is the process of successfully adapting to difficult or challenging life experiences, especially through mental, emotional and behavioral flexibility and adjustment to external and internal demands.

Resilience in leadership is having perseverance, determination, stick-to-it-ivness and grit, which can be defined as firmness of character; indomitable spirit (Merriam Webster).

Angela Duckworth, a world leading expert on Grit, defined it as 'perseverance and passion for long-term goals.' Duckworth and her team developed the Grit-scale and found that juniors in Chicago public schools with the most grit were more likely to graduate from high school than their less gritty peers.

Dennis Green, a former American football coach said, *"The secret to success is to **start from scratch and keep on scratching.**"*

Winston Churchill, a former prime minister of the United Kingdom, gave a speech on 'One of the Secrets of Greatness' during his visit to Harrow School, his alma mater, in which he said, *"**Never give in**. Never give in. Never, never, never, never – in nothing, great or small, large or petty – never give in, except to convictions of honor and good sense. Never yield to force. **Never yield to the apparently overwhelming might of the enemy.**"*

Abraham Lincoln, one of the greatest American Presidents, demonstrated a high level of perseverance through many catastrophes and failures before he became the President of the United States America.

- Lincoln failed in business in 1831 and again in 1833.
- He was defeated for Illinois state legislator in 1832.
- His fiancée died in 1835.
- He had a nervous breakdown in 1836.
- In 1843 and '48, Lincoln ran for Congress and lost both times.

- His U.S. Senate aspirations were no better, losing in 1855 and '59. He ran for vice president in 1856 and lost.
- His wife, Mary Todd, had a medical condition that manifested in mental and emotional instability.
- He buried two of his four beloved sons.
- Finally, in 1860, Abraham Lincoln was elected president.

Like Lincoln's, your dreams are all within reach - as long as you never stop.

Leaders have a never-give-up spirit even in the face of failure. The great Winston Churchill said, ***"success is moving from one failure to the other without losing enthusiasm."***

Thomas Edison, the great American inventor and businessman said, ***"Many of life's failures are people who did not realize how close they were to success when they gave up."*** When interviewed about his famous failed light bulb experiments, he said, ***"I have not failed. I have just found 1,000 ways that won't work."*** He had a lot of experience with setbacks from childhood when as a four-year-old child, he went home from school one day with a note in his pocket from his teacher which read, *"Your Tommy is too stupid to learn, get him out of school."* With determination and grit, his mother responded, *"My Tommy is not too stupid to learn, I will teach him myself."* That Tommy, who had only three months of formal schooling, grew up to be the great inventor.

As a leader, you will encounter with all kinds of challenges, problems and difficulties but you must be a dealer in hope; you must have an unbreakable spirit and you must never give up.

Apostle Paul gave an account of the ordeals he faced for the sake of the Church without giving up in 1 Corinthians 11:25-30; *"Three times I was beaten with rods; once I was stoned; three times I was shipwrecked; a night and a day I have been in the deep; in journeys often, in perils of waters, in perils of robbers, in perils of my own countrymen, in perils of the Gentiles, in perils in the city, inperils in the wilderness, in perils in the sea, in perils among false brethren; in weariness and toil, in sleeplessness often, in hunger and thirst, in fastings often, in cold and nakedness— besides the other things, what comes upon me daily: my deep concern for all the churches. Who is weak, and I am not weak? Who is made to stumble, and I do not burn with indignation? If I must boast, I will boast in the things which concern my infirmity."*

A great spirit of resilience was exemplified by Jesus, this was detailed in Hebrews 12:2, *"looking unto Jesus, the author and finisher of our faith, who for the joy that was set before Him endured the cross, despising the shame, and has sat down at the right hand of the throne of God."*

Great leaders keep their eyes on the goal. They do not allow themselves to be distracted in any form by any challenge on the way, which are inevitable but they rise up to the challenges. It has been shown that leaders who rise up to challenges do far better and have more fulfilment than those who do not.

Mihaly Csikszentmihalyi, a Hungarian psychologist, did a research on the devastating impact of the World War II on people around him to study the conditions that lead to happiness in everyday life. He found that when the challenge and skill level of a person is low, it leads to apathy, when the challenge level is low and skill level is high, it leads to boredom, when the challenge level is high and skill level is low, there will be stress but when the challenge level and skill level are both high, there will be happiness which he described as flow. It is therefore not only important to be skilled as a leader but a leader must rise to the level of their challenge.

However, in reality, the challenges sometimes become quite overwhelming and in such instances, I practice the philosophy of calm. There are times when the stresses are so great that all I can just do is cry or look for a trusted friend to share with. Most times, I find solace in praying and calling upon God as Abraham Lincoln said, ***"I have been driven many times upon my knees by the overwhelming conviction that I had nowhere else to go.*** *My own wisdom and that of all of me seemed insufficient for that day".*

I strongly believe that you cannot truly be a great leader if everything you experience is success after success. I remember one of my leadership struggles, we were building an edifice in our local community. The building comprised of a big hall and an office complex with three floors. We invited a civil engineer, an architect and a structural engineer to evaluate the project. Unfortunately, we were advised to pull down certain aspects of the building and erect new pillars for reinforcement. That advice came as a deep blow to me as we had invested millions into the project and I went home totally discouraged. I went on my knees in prayer and wept, after which I felt strongly within me that the problem at hand was going to work together for our good just as the Scriptures says. Armed with this word, we pulled down that part of the building and started construction again. At the end of the day, we achieved a very solid structure that has been standing firmly for many years now.

Sometimes as a leader you, may have failed and this may be as a result of a faulty process of leadership or moral failure but when one fails, one should avoid covering it up. Rather, one must confront the issue, make the necessary disclosure and try to adjust one's life. It is a defining point in life to ask oneself salient questions of one's ability to lead people and lead them well. There is always a second chance for leaders who in humility realize their failures and use it as a means of advancement rather than taking it as an adversity.

four

EFFECTIVE LEADERS FIND THEIR NICHE AND THEIR PLACE

(PEOPLE, PLACE, PURPOSE, PASSION)

Leadership is a calling in which God places you in a particular location per time. So, you must locate the right people, place, purpose and passion to serve.

Albert Schweitzer, a German theologian once said, *"I don't know what your destiny will be but one thing I do know,* ***the only ones among you who will be really happy are those who have sought and found how to serve."***

A leader knows that greatness is not about one's small world but about the larger community one influences. One can make the best of one's current location and move the world. It was said of Jesus that He came for every kind of people *"Is he the God of the Jews only? is he not also of the Gentiles? Yes, of the Gentiles also"* (Romans 3:29).

Jim Collins described one of the characteristics of those who achieve and sustain great results in his book "Good to Great" He wrote ***'to influence the world, you must know what you are deeply passionate about,*** *what you can be best in the world at and what best drives your economic and resource engine'.*

Jesus clearly expressed knowledge of His mission when He spoke to His disciples who were trying to send away a woman, whom they felt was unworthy, from Him, *"But he answered and said, I am not sent but unto the lost sheep of the house of Israel"* (Matthew 15:24). He said in John 4:34, *"My food is to do the will of Him who sent Me, and to finish His work."*

The Japanese Ikigai concept of what you love, what you are good at, what the world needs and what you can get paid for, is also a good tool for defining purpose in life and leadership. Leaders who will do greater works must understand their assignment and the reason for their existence. As Mark Twain said that, ***"the two most important days of your life are the day you are born and the day you figure out why".***

Simon Sinek, the best-selling author of "Start with Why" said, *"Every organization knows what they do which is the products or services they offer,* ***some organizations know***

how they do it but very few organizations know why they do what they do." He said further that what really matters is not what you do but the reason for which you do it. If you want to be a great leader and if you want people to follow you, you must be clear about your purpose and your 'why'.

Every assignment, gift or mandate demands a sense of purpose and urgency as the great Solomon wisely said in Ecclesiastes 3:1, *"To everything there is a season, and a time to every purpose under the heaven:"*

Understand that there is an appropriate time for what God wants you to do. To attain greatness, know your God, time and season; know what you should do and do it. Greatness is not just about being the first, it is about getting to your goals in life and attaining the height God has set for you.

five

EFFECTIVE LEADERS LEAD BY EXAMPLE

A leader leads the way, shows the way and in fact, is the way. James Kouzes in his book "The Leadership Challenge" highlighted that one most distinguishing characteristic of a great leaders is the model they make. Many researches have found out that one of the most important things that motivate people is not so much what a leader says but the leader's behaviour. Influence is from the medieval Latin word **"influentia",** that is, to flow into or get caught up.

Great leadership is about influencing others and not about displaying affluence as Paul said in 1 Peter 5:3, *"Not lording it over those entrusted to you, but being examples to the flock."* Jesus also said in Matthew 20:27-28, *"And let whosoever desires to be first among you, let him be your slave- just as the*

Son of Man did not come to be served, but to serve, and to give His life a ransom for many". John 13:15 says, *"I have set you an example that you should do as I have done for you".* Paul further said, *"Imitate me, just as I also imitate Christ"* (1 Corinthians 11:1). He also said in 1 Timothy 4:12, *"Let no man despise thy youth; but be thou an example of the believers, in word, in conversation, in charity, in spirit, in faith, in purity."*

In reality, it is the example a leader sets that the people will follow. A great leader is like a city set on a hill; a clock by which others regulate their watches. As a leader, you cannot say, "do as I say, not as I do". Ken Kesey, an American novelist said, *"You don't lead by pointing and telling people some place to go.* ***You lead by going to that place and making a case."*** Our life is the message; our voice is the echo and our examples are so contagious that our words are often not necessary. William Ward, the pioneer Baptist missionary said, *"The mediocre teacher tells. The good teacher explains. The superior teacher demonstrates. The great teacher inspires."*

One must first see the life one hopes to build as a leader. Titus 1:7-9 says, *"For a bishop must be blameless, as the steward of God; not self-willed, not soon angry, not given to wine, no striker, not given to filthy lucre; But a lover of hospitality, a lover of good men, sober, just, holy, temperate;*

Holding fast the faithful word as he hath been taught, that he may be able by sound doctrine both to exhort and to convince the gainsayers."

From my personal experience as a lecturer in the medical school, as a pastor of a local church and as a minister of the word of God, I have found out that people rarely quote my achievements but they often talk about how I have related to them emotionally and stood with them when they faced difficult situations. It has become apparent to me that the examples I show determine how much people will respect my words and follow me on my leadership journey. I have concluded that modelling the way is really the way of good leadership.

I remember our early days as we struggled to build a local church, we needed several thousands of dollars for the project and the money was not forthcoming. There were very few of us who were working at the time and we were not even on big salaries. I asked myself what I could do to get the resources we needed and it occurred to me that I must first model the way. So, I took a loan, emptied my bank account and gave all the money I had for the project. I did not give with the intention of receiving the money back but I simply believed in the project and that it was achievable. I realized that over time, many people responded to my act of faith and the project was successfully completed.

There are practical examples of people in the Bible who led by example that we can learn from.

- ## NEHEMIAH

Nehemiah 2:17-18, *"Then I said to them, "You see the distress that we are in, how Jerusalem lies waste, and its gates are burned with fire. Come and let us build the wall of Jerusalem, that we may no longer be a reproach." And I told them of the hand of my God which had been good upon me, and also of the king's words that he had spoken to me. So they said, "Let us rise up and build." Then they set their hands to this good work."*

Nehemiah 5:14-18; *"Moreover, from the time that I was appointed to be their governor in the land of Judah, from the twentieth year until the thirty-second year of King Artaxerxes, twelve years,* ***neither I nor my brothers ate the governor's provisions.*** *But the former governors who were before me laid burdens on the people, and took from them bread and wine, besides forty shekels of silver. Yes, even their servants bore rule over the people,* ***but I did not do so,*** *because of the fear of God. Indeed, I also continued the work on this wall, and we did not buy any land. All my servants were gathered there for the work. And at my table were one hundred and fifty Jews and rulers, besides those who came to us from the nations around us. Now that which was prepared daily was one ox and six choice sheep. Also fowl were prepared for me, and once every ten days an* *abundance of all kinds of wine.* ***Yet in spite of this I did not demand the governor's provisions, because the bondage was heavy on this people."***

- ## JOSHUA

Joshua 24: 14-15, **"***Now therefore fear the LORD, and serve him in sincerity and in truth: and put away the gods which your fathers served on the other side of the flood, and in Egypt; and serve ye the LORD. And if it seem evil unto you to serve the LORD, choose you this day whom ye will serve; whether the gods which your fathers served that were on the other side of the flood, or the gods of the Amorites, in whose land ye dwell:* ***but as for me and my house, we will serve the LORD."***

- ## MOSES

Hebrews 11:24-25, *"By faith Moses, when he was come to years, refused to be called the son of Pharaoh's daughter;*

25 *Choosing rather to suffer affliction with the people of God, than to enjoy the pleasures of sin for a season;*

- ## PAUL

Galatians 2:11-14, *"Now when Peter had come to Antioch, I withstood him to his face, because he was to be blamed; for before certain men came from James, he would eat with the Gentiles; but when they came, he withdrew and separated himself, fearing those who were of the circumcision. And the rest of the Jews also played the hypocrite with him, so that even Barnabas was carried away with their hypocrisy. But when I saw that they were not straightforward about the truth of the gospel, I said to Peter before them all,* ***"If you, being a Jew, live in the manner of Gentiles and not as the Jews, why do you compel Gentiles to live as Jews?"***

Samuel, the great prophet of God said in 1 Samuel 12:3, *"Here I am. Witness against me before the LORD and before His anointed: Whose ox have I taken, or whose donkey have I taken, or whom have I cheated? Whom have I oppressed, or from whose hand have I received any bribe with which to blind my eyes? I will restore it to you."*

This contrasts with many politicians of our days and even many people who profess and proclaim the gospel of Christ. We have become so centered on ourselves rather than modelling Christ to the people.

There is an interesting account of a certain woman who was upset about her son eating too much sugar. Despite her efforts to stop him, he continued to indulge in it and out of frustration she took him to see his hero, Mahatma Gandhi. She pleaded with him to speak with her son and make him stop eating sugar but he asked them to go home and return in two weeks. She went back home confused but returned with her son after two weeks as instructed. Gandhi looked directly at the boy and said to him *"Boy, you should stop eating sugar, it is not good for your health".* The boy promised to stop immediately. Then the mother turned to Gandhi and asked why he did not tell the boy to stop when they visited two weeks earlier. Gandhi smiled and replied the mother, *"two weeks ago, I was still eating sugar myself".*

Leading by example is a lot more effective than dishing out instructions as Alexandre Dumas, the prolific French writer said, *"Instruction is good but example is worth more"* and Todd Stocker, a clergy life coach said, *"Serving is the best kind of leading". "People are inspired by action. So, when it comes to charity work and leadership, leaders should always remember that it is a lot easier to encourage others on your team to join in on an effort if they see you doing it"* - Germany Kent (American journalist and philanthropist).

six

EFFECTIVE LEADERS KNOW THEIR LIMITS

We all have different potentials and capabilities. An effective leader does not try to be a jack of all trades; leaders find their unique serving potential and stay on it. 1 Corinthians 7:20 says, *"Let every man abide in the same calling wherein he was called."*

Great leaders stay on course and harness other people's potentials to help move the institution forward. Socrates, the great ancient Greek philosopher once said, ***"To know thyself is the beginning of wisdom".*** Paul wrote in 2 Corinthians 10:14-15, *"For we stretch not ourselves beyond our measure, as though we reached not unto you: for we are come as far as to you also in preaching the gospel of Christ: Not boasting of things without our measure, that is, of other men's labours; but having hope, when your faith is increased, that we shall be enlarged by you according to our rule abundantly."*

You must realize that what is for everybody might not be for you. Leaders know their potential and do not try to be someone else but focus on what God has given them to do. Pursuing goals are good but don't let it squeeze the life out of you. You must know God's plan for your life and what He wants you to do. Do what you ought to do and let God handle the rest.

Everyone of us has a unique calling given to us by God and effective leadership cannot come without endowment from above. In leadership, God is the pump and you are the pipe. When you decide to be the pump, you will run dry. One cannot succeed as a leader without total dependence upon God.

Romans 12:3 says, *"For I say, through the grace given unto me, to every man that is among you, not to think of himself more highly than he ought to think; but to think soberly, according as God hath dealt to every man the measure of faith."* John 15:4-5 says, *"Abide in Me, and I in you. As the branch cannot bear fruit of itself, unless it abides in the vine, neither can you, unless you abide in Me. "I am the vine, you are the branches. He who abides in Me, and I in him, bears much fruit; for without Me you can do nothing."* 1 Samuel 2:9 says, *"He will keep the feet of his saints, and the wicked shall be silent in darkness; for by strength shall no man prevail."*

A man once told the great Winston Churchill that he was a self-made man. He replied that by his statement, he had made God irrelevant.

Every one of us has our own values which must be sought out and we must find where we fit into God's plan. We must try to stay within the boundaries of our faith, our own domain, our area of ministry, our sphere of influence and the limits set by God for us. This does not mean you cannot rise above to do extraordinary things in life but you must know your limits, your gifting, your potentials and your abilities. Wherever we are lacking in abilities, God fills the gap and brings people around us to support us to fulfil our mission.

seven

EFFECTIVE LEADERS ARE ALWAYS LEARNING

"*The best leaders are constant learners*" (Harvard Business School).

According to Deepak Bhagat, a digital transformation strategist, ***"A remarkable leader is one who is continually seeking knowledge, growth and is committed to constant learning.*** *A great leader can always be spotted with smart folks gaining knowledge, sharing experiences and discussing ideas."*

As a leader, you must yearn for knowledge constantly. There is a vast supply of knowledge available in the world; if you seek after it, your learning curve will never be flat. Try to learn something new as you go along on your leadership journey through books and every environment you find yourself in. Leaders do not isolate themselves from people.

Leaders learn from the illiterate as well as the educated, the good as well as the bad.

Proverbs 18:15 says, *"The heart of the prudent getteth knowledge; and the ear of the wise seeketh knowledge."* Proverbs 19:27 (CEV) says, *"If you stop learning, you will forget what you already know".*

Proverbs 4:18, *"But the path of the just is as the shining light, that shineth more and more unto the perfect day."*

It takes constant learning to be a great leader. You must aim to know something about everything, everything about something and never leave the school of learning.

Michelangelo, a great Italian sculptor, painter, architect and engineer said when he was about 87 years old and working on St. Peter's Basilica, ***"I am still learning."*** Rick Warren, the author of the best seller, 'The purpose Driven Life', wrote, *"All leaders are learners. The moment you stop learning, you stop leading. I learn as much as I can, from as many as I can, as often as I can."* John F. Kennedy, the 35th President of the United States said, ***"Leadership and learning are indispensable to each other."***

When Apostle Paul was about to be sent to prison, he asked for his books and parchments in 2 Timothy 4:13, *"Bring the cloak that I left with Carpus at Troas when you come—and the books, especially the parchments."* He also advised Timothy saying, *"Study to shew thyself approved unto God, a workman that needeth not to be ashamed, rightly dividing the word of truth"* (2 Timothy 2:15). The great Solomon told us about the great preacher in Ecclesiastes 12:9-10, *"And moreover, because the Preacher was wise, he still taught the people knowledge; yes, he pondered and sought out and set in order many proverbs. The Preacher sought to find acceptable words; and what was written was upright—words of truth."*

Don't just stay in your comfort zone, grow up and keep learning. John Wesley, the great Anglican clergyman said, ***"Once in seven years I burn all my sermons;*** *for it is a shame if I cannot write better sermons now than I did seven years ago."*

Art Linkletter, the famous motivational speaker and author said, ***"I never want to be what I want to be, because there's always something out there yet for me.*** *I get a kick out of living in the here and now but I never want to feel I know the best way how. There's always one hill higher, with a better view; something waiting to be learned that I never knew. Till my days are over, never fully fill my cup; let me go on growing up."*

As you continue to learn and increase in knowledge, don't fall into the error of confusing the word "mastery" with perfection. Perfection is an ongoing process and the only perfect Being is God.

eight

EFFECTIVE LEADERS DEMONSTRATE LOVE

Leadership is about love. I have come to find out that leadership is really about the people and not the leader. You cannot be a great leader until you can really love others and oftentimes that love is reciprocated by the people. Loving people sometimes comes at a great price. As a leader, you must be prepared to suffer hurt from the very people you show love to but your duty is to love without expecting reciprocity.

In my leadership journey, I have found out that no matter what you do, you will find people who will slander you, speak evil of you and criticize you unjustly. The options available are to either be bitter, take revenge and fight back (which are quite tempting) or to continue loving inspite of it all. Over time I have found out that to be a great leader, one must have a very strong endurance capacity. You must persevere and accept that it is your duty to love but you cannot control people's reactions to the love you show them.

So, on such occasions, I have had to model Christ *"Who, when he was reviled, reviled not again; when he suffered, he threatened not; but committed himself to him that judgeth righteously"* (1 Peter 2:23). Over time, these critics disappeared and their slanderous statements were found to be false. Leaders must keep their eyes on the mission and not allow themselves be distracted by people's reactions as Abraham Lincoln said, *"If I care to listen to every criticism, let alone act on them, then this shop may as well be closed for all other businesses.* ***I have learned to do my best, and if the end result is good then I do not care for any criticism,*** *but if the end result is not good, then even the praise of ten angels would not make the difference."*

Love is indeed very crucial in leadership, that is why Jesus led by love when He was on earth. John 13:1 says, *"Having loved His own who were in the world, He loved them to the end".* He also ensured that Simon was a man of love before He gave him the responsibility of leading the church. In John 21:15, He said *"So when they had eaten breakfast, Jesus said to Simon Peter, "Simon, son of Jonah, do you love me more than these?" He said to Him, "Yes, Lord; You know that I love You." He said to him, "Feed my lambs."*

I always encourage everyone who desires to be a great leader to read the magnificent chapter of 1 Corinthians 13 again and again, if not every day, at least once a week. That would help to set the tone for effective leadership. One should particularly take note of verses 4-6 which say, *"love is patient and kind, love does not envy or boast, is not arrogant or rude. It does not insist on its own way. It is not irritable or resentful. It does not rejoice at wrong doing but rejoices with the truth. Love bears all things, believes all things, hopes all things, endures all things".* A very high level of importance is placed on love as 1 Corinthians 13:13 says, *"And now abideth faith, hope, charity, these three; but the greatest of these is charity."*

I have found that sometimes in leadership, I may have to give up my power to exercise authority over people and submit and just love people for who they are.

Love in leadership is bi-directional. Not only must one love the people one leads, the people must also love the leader as Paul said in 1 Thessalonians 5:12-13, *"And we beseech you, brethren, to know them which labour among you, and are over you in the Lord, and admonish you; And to esteem them very highly in love for their work's sake. And be at peace among yourselves."*

Love in leadership is sacrificial and does not wait for reciprocity. Paul said in 2 Corinthians 12:15, *"And I will very gladly spend and be spent for you; though the more abundantly I love you, the less I be loved."*

One of the great challenges of great leaders is that they must learn to love their enemies and avoid bitterness. It is difficult to like our enemies but it is possible to love them through the grace of God. Every one that will be used of God must come to the point where they are able to love their enemies. If a leader is bitter, it spreads to the whole team as Hebrews 12:15 says, *"Looking diligently lest any man fail of the grace of God; lest any root of bitterness springing up trouble you, and thereby many be defiled".*

Jesus instructed us in Luke 6:27-28 that, *"But I say unto you which hear, Love your enemies, do good to them which hate you, Bless them that curse you, and pray for them which despitefully use you."* Paul also warned the Roman church in Romans 12:20 saying, *"Therefore "If your enemy is hungry, feed him; If he is thirsty, give him a drink; For in so doing you will heap coals of fire on his head."*

I am particularly intrigued by Justin Chadwick, an English actor and film producer's popular movie, 'Long Walk to Freedom', which gave an account of Nelson Mandela's early life, coming of age, education and twenty-seven years in prison before becoming the president of South Africa. During an interview of Mandela in the movie, he was asked a question about the possibility of him taking revenge on those who had ill-treated him and his response was quite inspiring. He said, *"I admit, I want revenge but I want something more than that; that is, to* ***live without fear and hatred."*** This response was remarkable in that he openly acknowledged his natural human instinct to seek revenge but his paramount aspiration as a leader was for something far better.

One of the twentieth century's greatest political and spiritual leaders, Mahatma Gandhi said, ***"An eye for an eye will leave the whole world blind."***

There is an inspiring and heartrending account of a man, Gordon Wilson and his daughter, Marie who were regrettably caught in the carnage that followed the detonation of a bomb by the Irish Republican Army in 1987. As they both lay trapped under the rubble, Wilson held his daughter's hand and comforted her as she was dying. Her last words to him were, *"Daddy, I love you very much"*. When he was interviewed by the BBC after the incident, Wilson said, *"I* ***bear no ill will, I bear no grudge.*** *Dirty sort of talk is not going to bring her back to life. She was a great wee lassie. She loved her profession. She was a pet. She's dead. She's in* *heaven and we shall meet again. I will pray for these men tonight and every night."*

Jonathan Bardon, a historian commented on Wilson's words and said, *"No words in more than twenty-five years of violence in Northern Ireland had such a powerful emotional impact."*

Wilson went on afterwards to help launch a community outreach program which has helped young people in Northern Ireland to participate in international programmes and gave bursaries to promote reconciliation in Northern Ireland.

Jesus Christ demonstrated the power more than anyone else to love our enemies when he was crucified, spat upon and reviled, He said *"Father forgive them, for they do not know what they do"* (Luke 23:34). Great leaders must learn to forgive their enemies and turn them to friends.

nine

EFFECTIVE LEADERS LAY DOWN THEIR LIVES FOR A CAUSE

You cannot be a great leader if you do not make sacrifices for a cause or the people you lead. Jesus stated this clearly, He said, *"I am the good shepherd: the good shepherd giveth his life for the sheep."* (John 10:11). Good leaders move from their comfort zones to their challenge zone and gives all they can for the progress of the people. We can see this sacrificial leadership in the life of Esther when the existence of her people was threatened in Esther 4:16 where she said *"Go, gather together all the Jews that are present in Shushan, and fast ye for me, and neither eat nor drink three days, night or day: I also and my maidens will fast likewise; and so will I go in unto the king, which is not according to the law: and if I perish, I perish."*

Moses sacrificed his lofty position as a prince as we read in Hebrews 11: 24-26, *"By faith Moses, when he was come to years, refused to be called the son of Pharaoh's daughter;* ***Choosing rather to suffer affliction with the people of God, than to enjoy the pleasures of sin for a season;*** *Esteeming the reproach of Christ greater riches than the treasures in Egypt: for he had respect unto the recompence of the reward.*

Jesus Christ is our greatest model of a sacrificial leader *"Who gave himself a ransom for all, to be testified in due time"* (1 Timothy 2:6).

The early Christians, including Stephen, James, Peter, Paul and others were among the most tragic examples of people who sacrificed everything for a cause. Most of them were tortured, burnt to death, boiled in oil, beheaded, crucified and even fed to lions for sport.

Apostle Paul said in 2 Corinthians 12:14-15, *"Behold, the third time I am ready to come to you; and I will not be burdensome to you: for I seek not yours, but you: for the children ought not to lay up for the parents, but the parents for the children. And I will very gladly spend and be spent for you; though the more abundantly I love you, the less I be loved."* He said further in Romans 9:1-3, *"I say the truth in Christ, I lie not, my conscience also bearing me witness in the Holy Ghost, That I have great heaviness and continual sorrow in my heart. For I could wish that myself were accursed from Christ for my brethren, my kinsmen according to the flesh:"*

Mahatma Gandhi, one of the greatest political and spiritual leaders in history, led the fight for Indian nationalism against the British rule in the 1920s and was assassinated at the age of 78 years.

Mother Theresa, a Roman Catholic nun, lived a life of total sacrifice. She was dedicated to caring for the poor, sick, orphaned and dying. She founded the Missionaries of Charity in India which has currently spread to over 130 countries.

Nelson Mandela, the first black president of South Africa, was an anti-apartheid revolutionary and a notable human rights activist. He had the option of keeping quiet but he chose to lead the entire South African nation against racial segregation and apartheid. He was convicted of sabotage and conspiracy to overthrow the government and was sentenced to life imprisonment. He eventually served twenty-seven years in prison after an international campaign was launched for his freedom and later went on to become the president of South Africa.

Reverend Martin Luther King Jr., the most famous civil rights leader in American history, led a powerful movement against racial inequality despite many threats to his life. His bravery and dedication to the cause for equal human rights led to his assassination in 1968.

Lieutenant John Robert Fox, an American artillery officer died in the line of duty while he held on to his oath to serve and protect. He called for artillery fire on their German enemies very close to his own position in order to give his troops a chance to win the battle at the expense of his own life.

Liu Xiaobo, famously referred to as “China's Nelson Mandela”, audaciously spoke against the Communist regime in China which led to his imprisonment for 16 years.

Great leaders do not seek their own comfort but they break out of their comfort zone and risk everything, including their lives, for the people. A great leader cannot afford to be selfish or self-centered. Leadership is really not about the leader but about the people; Leaders build people up and do not use the apparatus of leadership to exploit them for acquisition of wealth and fame. An exploitative leader may grow fast but cannot go far, as it is often said and such a one's legacy will not stand the test of time.

ten

EFFECTIVE LEADERS TAKE LEAPS OF FAITH

Faith is daring; it is getting out of the comfort zone, believing against all odds and it is the basis of great achievements. The Bible describes faith as, *"the substance of things hoped for, the evidence of things not seen. For by it the elders obtained a good report"* (Hebrews 11:1-2).

Great leaders have a high risk quotient (faith) and not just a great intelligence quotient. They take people from where they are to where they ought to be without fear - which is a risk. They are people of faith who question the status quo and refuse to be victims of circumstances. Leaders do not act at the level of their convenience but at their level of commitment.

We can learn faith from certain great leaders in the Bible:

CALEB silenced the people of Israel who were afraid to go into the promised land because of the negative report they received from the spies who had gone ahead into the land. In Numbers 13:30 we read, *"Then Caleb silenced the people before Moses and said 'We should go up and take possession of the land, for we can certainly do it'.*

ABRAHAM was told by God to leave his own country to another land he didn't know and *"By faith Abraham, when he was called to go out into a place which he should after receive for an inheritance, obeyed; and he went out, not knowing whither he went."* (Hebrews 11:8). He took a great risk of faith.

ESTHER took a great risk at the expense of her life to approach the king in order to plead for the lives of her people which was an offence punishable by death. Esther 4:16 says, *"Go, gather together all the Jews that are present in Shushan, and fast ye for me, and neither eat nor drink three days, night or day: I also and my maidens will fast likewise; and so will I go in unto the king, which is not according to the law: and if I perish, I perish."* Her expression was a profound display of faith.

GIDEON led a war against an army of 120,000 men with just 300 men by faith in God. Judges 7:7 says, *"Then the Lord said to Gideon, "By the three hundred men who lapped I will save you, and deliver the Midianites into your hand. Let all the other people go, every man to his place."*

DAVID challenged the Philistine without weapons of war but with faith in God. 1 Samuel 17:45-47 says, *"Then said David to the Philistine, Thou comest to me with a sword, and with a spear, and with a shield: but I come to thee in the name of the LORD of hosts, the God of the armies of Israel, whom thou hast defied. This day will the LORD deliver thee into mine hand; and I will smite thee, and take thine head from thee; and I will give the carcases of the host of the Philistines this day unto the fowls of the air, and to the wild beasts of the earth; that all the earth may know that there is a God in Israel. And all this assembly shall know that the LORD saveth not with sword and spear: for the battle is the LORD'S, and he will give you into our hands."*

To carry out the mandate of God, we must exercise faith. The whole essence of the gospel of salvation becomes mere history without the instrumentality of faith. You actualize your destiny by your faith; except you believe it, you will not see it. You must learn to give God full control by faith and damn the consequences.

I once faced a great challenge when I was appointed as the editor-in chief of a medical journal that seemed to have ground to a halt. I needed faith to take the giant step of reviving the journal; this seemed like an almost impossible task. After a period of forging ahead in spite of the challenges, we were able to restore the journal to the point of publishing regularly and even getting it to some level of good international standing.

I also remember the many experiences I had while building our church in a locality that had no substantial credit facility and where the people were not very wealthy. I had to take a huge risk to build the edifice, relying solely on faith in God, taking the first step and then forging ahead.

eleven

EFFECTIVE LEADERS PRODUCE RESULTS AND LEAVE ENDURING LEGACIES

Good leadership is not measured by the many positions or offices one has held; this is why the curriculum vitae is very deceptive. The evidence of leadership is about outcome, having measurable accomplishments, taking the people to the next level, meeting deadlines and effective execution of tasks. To achieve results, you must have smart goals. Great leaders are creative, they question the status quo and don't just blend in with the crowd.

Results of leadership are measured by impact factor – How has your leadership impacted the people or organization you lead? What legacy have you left behind? When you leave a position, what people say of you?

True greatness lies in impacting lives and leaving a legacy that outlives the leader. A true legacy is something that is worth buying into and following even when the leader is no longer around. It is about producing results that are enduring and motivating those you lead to produce even more.

Mordecai was a man who left an enduring legacy behind and he was praised for his good deeds in Esther 10:3 which says, *"For Mordecai the Jew was next unto king Ahasuerus, and great among the Jews, and accepted of the multitude of his brethren, seeking the wealth of his people, and speaking peace to all his seed."*

Martin Luther King led peaceful protests in his fight for the civil rights of African Americans, the economically disadvantaged and victims of injustice. He left an enduring legacy of pushing for landmark legislations in the United States of America such as the Civil Rights Acts and Voting Rights Act. His legacy was rewarded with a Nobel Peace Prize and a federal holiday in the USA since 1986.

Nelson Mandela, former president of South Africa, made a significant mark in the history of South Africa and in fact the world history through his fight to break the hold of apartheid in the nation, bringing liberty to the black population in South Africa.

Abraham Lincoln, the 16th president of the United States of America, literally brought an end to slavery in the nation when he issued the emancipation proclamation to free slaves after a long battle with antagonists. He was also instrumental to preventing a secession in the country and winning the civil war.

William Wilberforce, a British politician and philanthropist, passionately fought for the antislavery legislation to be passed in England. He also ensured that emancipation of slaves was enacted into law despite much opposition.

Steve Jobs, the co-founder of Apple Inc., pioneered the evolution of the personal computer era and launched groundbreaking products in the world of telecommunications. His goal was to get a computer in the hands of everyday people and he did just that; a mission which has outlived him.

The greatest questions of leadership are, "what did you do, what will be said of you after you are gone and what will you be remembered for?" As Sheryl Sandberg, the Chief Operating Officer of Facebook said, *"**Leadership is about making others better as a result of your presence** and making sure that impact lasts in your absence".* Revelations 14:13b says, *"Yea, saith the Spirit, that they may rest from their labours; and their works do follow them."*

When your leadership tenure is over, you should be able to say like Paul said in 2 Timothy 4:7, *"I have fought a good fight, I have finished my course, I have kept the faith."*

twelve

EFFECTIVE LEADERS ARE TEAM PLAYERS

(THEY RALLY THE TROOPS)

Team building is the process of bringing in like-minded persons to contribute individually to a shared vision. Rallying the troops means to organize people for a common goal, interest or a cause and instill energy and enthusiasm into them.

Andrew Carnegie, one of the captains of industry of 19th century America said, ***"Teamwork is the ability to work together towards a common vision.*** *The ability to direct individual accomplishments toward organizational objectives. It is the fuel that allows common people to attain uncommon results."*

All over history, leadership has never been a one-man affair. There is no way a leader can succeed if he does not understand the principles of teamwork. Teamwork brings unity but unity is not uniformity, rather, it is diversity.

Jesus Christ built teams among His disciples, *"And he called unto him the twelve, and began to send them forth by two and two; and gave them power over unclean spirits" (Mark 6:7).* He *"...appointed other seventy also, and sent them two and two before his face into every city and place, whither he himself would come"* (Luke 10:1).

At the inception of the Christian church, the Apostles showed unity as they *"were all with one accord in one place. And suddenly there came a sound from heaven as of a rushing mighty wind, and it filled all the house where they were sitting. And there appeared unto them cloven tongues like as of fire, and it sat upon each of them. And they were all filled with the Holy Ghost, and began to speak with other tongues, as the Spirit gave them utterance"* (Acts 2:1-4). Paul admonished to us to keep *"Endeavouring to keep the unity of the Spirit in the bond of peace"* (Ephesians 4:3).

Jesus, knowing the power of unity, focused on it in His last prayer for the church in John 17:21, *"That they all may be one; as thou, Father, art in me, and I in thee, that they also may be one in us: that the world may believe that thou hast sent me."* He prayed for unity of the church because when there is unity, there is strength. Little wonder the present church is not as formidable and strong because of the diversity and differences among us.

The wise Solomon also said, *"Two are better than one; because they have a good reward for their labour. For if they fall, the one will lift up his fellow: but woe to him that is alone when he falleth; for he hath not another to help him up. Again, if two lie together, then they have heat: but how can one be warm alone? And if one prevail against him, two shall withstand him; and a threefold cord is not quickly broken."* (Ecclesiastes 4:9-12).

One great illustration of the power of team spirit can be found in the Bible when a group people were trying to build a tower that would reach the heavens. "And the LORD said, *"Indeed the people are one and they all have one language, and this is what they begin to do; now nothing that they propose to do will be withheld from them"* (Genesis 11:6).

Henry Ford, founder of Ford Motor Company who revolutionized factory production said, *"Coming together is a beginning, keeping together is progress,* ***working together is success****"*.

John Doerr, an American investor said, *"Ideas are easy, but execution is everything.* ***It takes a team to win."***

Building a formidable team involves:

a. **Cohesion -** forming a united front.

b. **Conflict resolution –** taking the effort to understand perspectives of opposing individuals and groups to bring about a peaceful solution to their disputes.

c. **Maximizing competencies –** using the collective input of multiple people to achieve a common goal.

Bruce Tuckman, an educational psychologist, postulated that all groups go through distinct stages of forming, storming, norming and perfecting as they develop. He further said that *"while all troops go through the process, those who do so consciously and deliberately will be the most successful. Those that don't are the most likely to die."* In forming a team, we must be aware of those who do not flow with the team's spirit and know how to handle them wisely lest their actions completely destroy the common goal.

Effective leaders must welcome criticism; they should even be prepared for conflict but they must be able to resolve it amicably and be quick to dissociate from people who just want to create divisions and disrupt the harmony of the institution. As Paul wrote in Romans 16:17, *"Now I urge you, brethren, note those who cause divisions and offenses, contrary to the doctrine which you learned, and avoid them."*

Beyond working with a team towards a common goal, the leader must avoid acting like a super-human around team members. Leaders should have people whom they can confide in, be authentic with and be vulnerable with; those who can pray with, counsel and support them.

As a pastor of a local church with a very busy schedule, I meet with a group of people once a week. They are not so much ministers but regular people who care about me and about my mission. When we meet once a week to share together and pray, I find myself being able to open up to them about my struggles and challenges. There are instances when they have no solution to offer but they simply weep with me and pray with me. I have often found that after even a short period of prayers, I receive strength.

My experience seems quite similar to the account of Jesus Christ when He was overwhelmed in the garden of Gethsemane and God intervened by sending angels to strengthen Him (Luke 22:39-44). A leader needs to have a team made up of people who help carry the weight (especially the emotional weight) of leadership.

PART TWO

PITFALLS OF EFFECTIVE LEADERSHIP

one

FAMILIARITY

According to the online dictionary, familiarity can be described as a state of having close acquaintance or relaxed friendship and intimacy with someone. The reality is that familiarity, as they say, breeds contempt, corrupts individuals, breeds conspirators and compromises an establishment. Be friendly but not familiar.

Leaders should know when to give space; no matter how close leaders are to the people, they must learn to create a healthy gap. Ecclesiastes 3:5b says there is, *"a time to embrace, and a time to refrain from embracing"*.

Moses' siblings, out of familiarity, despised him as a prophet of God in Numbers 12:2, *"And they said, Hath the LORD indeed spoken only by Moses? hath he not spoken also by us? And the LORD heard it.* The Lord instructed him in Exodus

24:1-2, *"And he said unto Moses, Come up unto the LORD, thou, and Aaron, Nadab, and Abihu, and seventy of the elders of Israel; and worship ye afar off.* ***And Moses alone shall come near the LORD****: but they shall not come nigh; neither shall the people go up with him."*

Our Lord Jesus Christ suffered the consequences of familiarity through His kinsmen because they knew His roots. We read in Mark 6:1-5, *"And he went out from thence, and came into his* ***own country****; and his disciples follow him. And when the sabbath day was come, he began to teach in the synagogue: and many hearing him were astonished, saying, From whence hath this man these things? and what wisdom is this which is given unto him, that even such mighty works are wrought by his hands?* ***Is not this the carpenter, the son of Mary, the brother of James, and Joses, and of Juda, and Simon? and are not his sisters here with us?*** *And they were offended at him. But Jesus said unto them,* ***A prophet is not without honour, but in his own country, and among his own kin, and in his own house.*** *And he could there do no mighty work, save that he laid his hands upon a few sick folk, and healed them."*

Familiarity breeds contempt; it leads to compromise, it contaminates your relationships, it corrupts your conscience, it leads to complications and it may cost you your life. Be wise, stay safe and be on your guard. Be friendly, associate feely but be firm on principles. John 2:24, says *"But Jesus did not commit Himself to them because he knew all men."*

Julia Ward, a 19th century American poet said, ***"Familiarity so dulls the edge of perception*** *as to make us least acquainted with things forming part of our daily lives."*

Familiarity will lead to distractions and distractions attract disaster. You must find your focus, set your boundaries, fulfil your calling and say a big 'NO' to distractions.

When you strive to satisfy everyone and be in everyone's good books, you will miss out on God. Herbert Swope, an American editor who won Pulitzer prizes said, *"I cannot give you the formula for success but I can give you the formula for failure, which is, Try to please everybody."* Max Lucado, the best-selling Christian author and Pastor wrote, ***"A man who wants to lead the orchestra must turn his back on the crowd."***

Do not make yourself so available to everyone, Proverbs 25:17 says, *"Withdraw thy foot from thy neighbour's house; lest he be weary of thee, and so hate thee."*

two

REFUSING TO KEEP FIT

You must have a daily agenda and daily habits for spiritual vitality, physical vitality and mental agility. Take right measures for self-care and develop a healthy productive capability/production balance proposed by Steven Covey in his book, '7 Habits of Highly Effective People'.

In order to be productive, you must improve your productive capability. To achieve results for the long-haul, you must keep yourself healthy, strengthened, and empowered. Ensure you have a "Me-time".

Keeping fit involves a healthy balance between work, play and recreation. You must find time to rest regularly and often. God exemplified this in Genesis 2:2, *"And on the seventh day God ended his work which he had made; and he rested on the seventh day from all his work which he had made."*

Your body houses your brain, your intelligence, your assets and your potentials. The level you will attain on earth depends on how much time you spend to keep fit and stay healthy. No matter your gifting, your body will determine how far you will go. A 19th century preacher, Robert Murray McCheyne, worked so hard that his health finally failed. He wrote before he died at the young age of 29 years, ***"God gave me a message to deliver and a horse to ride. Alas, I have killed the horse and now I cannot deliver the message."***

Are you overwhelmed with deadlines? Work at it, take it a day at a time but don't die before you get to the line. Do what you ought to do and let God handle the rest. Do you have a busy life? Please keep it in the balance. Pursuing goals are good but don't let it squeeze the life out of you. Regardless of the work, find rest for your soul, spirit and body. Take time to pause and gain perspective. Take time to stop all things and commune with yourself. Take time to fellowship with others; family, friends and even foes. Don't be too busy to neglect the business of life, which is joy that comes from a calm and serene soul.

One's emotional health as a leader is just as important as one's physical health. A great tool that can be used to recalibrate and achieve balance is the 'Wheel of Life', a concept originally designed by Paul J. Meyer, the founder of Success Motivation Institute Inc. This tool creates a graphical representation of each aspect of life and assesses what is off balance so that you can redirect your life to how you want it to be ordered to prevent frustration, excessive stress and burn out which can lead to depression.

It is highly imperative for a leader to maintain an all-round balance which is often difficult to achieve simultaneously but can be achieved sequentially. Leaders must learn to use the pause button in challenging situations so that their families will not be on the losing end of things.

Sometime ago, a series of interviews were conducted on some very successful pastors of local churches on how they achieved balance in their lives. They all claimed to be doing very well but when their spouses and children were interviewed for their perspective, it was discovered that these pastors were actually negligent of their families. This makes it quite obvious that it may sometimes be necessary for leaders to disengage from the rigorous activities of leadership and go on a holiday with their families to avoid being entrapped by the success syndrome.

It must also be noted that work is not synonymous with exercise. Unlike excessive work which generates stress, exercise helps to keep your thinking, learning and judgment skills sharp as you get older. It boosts energy, improves the mood, helps to combat health challenges and diseases and extends one's lifespan. Most of the great people in the world have inculcated exercise as part of their daily routine and I would like to highlight a few examples of leaders all over the world who keep fit.

1. John Chambers (Cisco CEO) jogs 5 miles daily.
2. Larry Ellison (Oracle CEO) is a slim 68years old who races sailboats and looks younger than his age.
3. Tim Cook (Apple CEO) is a fitness buff with great stamina. He hikes and cycles.
4. Dan King (CEO ReadyTalk) is known as world's fittest CEO. His company offers free yoga, massages and subsidized gym subscription for his employees. He said, *"**people taking care of themselves are going to have higher levels of energy** and are going to be more balanced in terms of work life".*
5. Barack Obama (former US president) works out every morning and plays basketball.
6. Mitt Romney (US senator) jogs daily.

three

REFUSING TO TAKE FEEDBACKS

Leadership is a covenant and a contract. It is responsibility for a community and compliance with procedures. In order to stay effective in leadership, it is important to seek feedback from your followers or subordinates. Socrates, the great philosopher said ***"An unexamined life is not worth living."***

Don't feel too big to ask the people you lead from time to time "How am I doing?" Jesus Christ often asked for feedbacks from His disciples as seen in Matthew 16:13 which says, *"When Jesus came into the coasts of Caesarea Philippi, he asked his disciples, saying, Whom do men say that I the Son of man am?"*

Never set yourself to be too big for correction, lest you be on the path to perdition as Proverbs 15:31-32 says, *"The ear that heareth the reproof of life abideth among the wise. He that refuseth instruction despiseth his own soul: but he that heareth reproof getteth understanding."*

You must learn to respond positively to criticism and use corrections as stepping stones to your advancement. Proverbs 19:20 says, *"Hear counsel, and receive instruction, that thou mayest be wise in thy latter end."* Proverbs 12:1 says, *"Whoso loveth instruction loveth knowledge: but he that hateth reproof is brutish."*

It is not enough for leaders to just seek honest feedback; they must surround themselves with people who are not afraid to give it. Proverbs 27:17 *says, "As iron sharpens iron, so a man sharpens the countenance of his friend."*

Feedbacks are very necessary as they help to recalibrate you, sharpen your skill and keep you on track. Proverbs 1:5, *"A wise man will hear, and will increase learning; and a man of understanding shall attain unto wise counsels:"* 1 Corinthians 9:27 says, *"But I keep under my body, and bring it into subjection: lest that by any means, when I have preached to others, I myself should be a castaway."*

I found the story of Alfred B. Nobel, known for the famous Nobel Prize, quite humbling. He was a 19th century inventor, scientist, manufacturer and businessman, who built his fortune from manufacturing dynamites. When Nobel's brother died, a French newspaper erroneously published it in the news as Alfred's obituary and wrote, *"The merchant of death is dead. Dr Alfred Nobel, who made his fortune by finding a way to kill more people faster than ever before, died yesterday."* Nobel was horrified when he read the what had been written about him. This motivated him to re-evaluate his contribution to humanity and establish the prestigious Nobel Prizes for literature, science, economics and peace which are awarded to those who have conferred the greatest benefit to mankind.

This account of Nobel shows the power of honest and timely feedback which is essential for leaders. Leaders should not believe that they can never be without fault but must continually examine themselves so as to become better leaders. Proverbs 12:15 says, *"The way of a fool is right in his own eyes: but he that hearkeneth unto counsel is wise."*

four

FAILURE TO CONNECT WITH SIGNIFICANT OTHERS

(MENTORS AND MENTEES)

Mentors are those who coach, and calibrate the careers of others. They encourage and build others up. A leader is not a stand-alone person; he must have mentors at all levels who would continually sharpen him. As Isaac Newton said, ***"If I have seen further, it is by standing on the shoulder of giants".***

No one can be a great leader who does not connect with mentors and shepherds. The truth is that you cannot outgrow your foundation. Find your root and be faithful to your foundations, without which you cannot stand against the storms for Psalms 11:3 says, *"If the foundations be destroyed, what can the righteous do?"*

Have you soon forgotten? – The mother who nurtured you, the father who provided for you, the siblings who encouraged you, the friends who cheered you on, the shepherds who took care of your soul, the institutions that educated you, the many lives that made you who you are. Forgetting is myopic; those who forget will one day regret. So, look back – is there one person to help, someone to say thank you to, someone to visit or call, someone to pray for? Just don't forget. Your greatness is the result of the inputs of many. Be humble and give thanks. Proverbs 22:28 says, *"Remove not the ancient landmark, which thy fathers have set."*

We must have accountability figures involved in our lives. We must submit to one another and report back to base as Ephesians 5:21 says, *"Submitting yourselves one to another in the fear of God.* 1 Corinthians 4:15 further says, *"For though ye have ten thousand instructors in Christ, yet have ye not many fathers: for in Christ Jesus I have begotten you through the gospel."*

John 15:4 says, *"Abide in me, and I in you. As the branch cannot bear fruit of itself, except it abide in the vine; no more can ye, except ye abide in me."*

five

FALLING INTO THE TEMPTATION TO BE FAKE

Being fake means to attempt to create an image that does not exist through manipulation and deception. Authenticity on the other hand is the quality of being real, genuine and true to self.

Integrity, honesty and sincerity are cardinal to great leadership; hence, great leaders must gird themselves with the belt of truth.

Leadership is not about being an actor, it is about truth and transparency. It is what you are in the dark when no one can see you. So, do not try to play the act, dress the act or speak the act. As a leader, you must decisively renounce the hidden things of deceitfulness. 2 Corinthians 4:2 says, *"But have renounced the hidden things of dishonesty, not walking in craftiness, nor handling the word of God deceitfully; but by manifestation of the truth commending ourselves to every man's conscience in the sight of God."*

Hypocrisy is self-delusion and a leader must avoid it absolutely. You must be totally genuine and transparent. Jesus gave many warnings about hypocrisy among certain leaders in the Bible. In Matthew 23:27-28 He said, *"Woe to you, scribes and Pharisees, hypocrites! For you are like whitewashed tombs which indeed appear beautiful outwardly, but inside are full of dead men's bones and all uncleanness. Even so you also outwardly appear righteous to men, but inside you are full of hypocrisy and lawlessness."* He said further in Matthew 7:15, *"Beware of false prophets, who come to you in sheep's clothing, but inwardly they are ravening wolves."*

As a true leader one should never hide one's vulnerabilities and must avoid putting up the façade of a perfect person. Leaders know their weaknesses but do not indulge them and are not double-faced. Luke 12:2 says, *"For there is nothing covered, that shall not be revealed; neither hid, that shall not be known."*

Sometimes, leaders struggle with pride, emotional attraction to the opposite sex, temptations to experiment with their instincts and so on. At such times, leaders should confront themselves rather than give excuses. To be forewarned is to be forearmed and as it is often said, prevention is better than cure. In extreme situations, this may necessitate a leader going for counselling or staying off leadership for a while in order to recalibrate. An honest talk with a counsellor, a genuine friend or even your spouse may be the beginning of restoration. Do not forget that a man's sin finds him out, so cover-ups do not last.

six

EGO AND PRIDE

Leadership is not about positions, programs, prosperity or the pride of men; it is about humility. Leadership is not about being the star but the servant. It is being on the same level as those you lead.

Pride and greatness are polar opposites. Pride is a sign that a person is going down and no proud person in the race of life finishes well, so learn to stay cool. If you desire to make a significant impact in life as a leader, don't even try to swallow your pride, spit it out. Ego has been defined as "Edging God Out" and it is important for great leaders to crucify their ego.

Proverbs 6:16-19 lists pride as one of *"These six things the LORD hates, Yes, seven are an abomination to Him: A proud look, A lying tongue, hands that shed innocent blood, a heart that devises wicked plans, feet that are swift in running to evil, a false witness who speaks lies, and one who sows discord among brethren."*

Saint Augustine, the ancient Christian teacher said, ***"It was pride that changed angels into devils; it is humility that makes men as angels."*** As a leader, humility is a virtue that will keep you on top but pride is a vice that leads to a fall. Do not build a tabernacle around your success and don't go about blowing your own horn when you have made good achievements. You must strive to maintain a humble disposition irrespective of your status or achievements. Always maintain a cool head and a sane mind. Proverbs 27:1-2 says, *"Do not boast about tomorrow, For you do not know what a day may bring forth. Let another man praise you, and not your own mouth; A stranger, and not your own lips."* Jesus Christ said, *"Take My yoke upon you and learn from Me, for I am gentle and lowly in heart, and you will find rest for your souls"* (Matthew 11:19).

As a leader, be careful of flatterers because they will dig your grave. Flattery kills even the best of us. Seek not human praise; too much praise may sink and derail you. Don't allow people praise you to pride and doom. Proverbs 29:5 says, *"A man that flattereth his neighbour spreadeth a net for his feet."*

Leaders should not, out of pride, insist on their ways, but must surround themselves with a team of experts to counsel them as they face the work. They must continually seek to do good, keep at it and let God alone be glorified.

seven

TAKING THINGS AND PEOPLE AT FACE VALUE

We often fall into the error of trusting people and giving our all to them without knowing who they truly are. Leaders must be careful of making assumptions about people or situations without asking the right questions about them. Be sure to verify and allow people prove themselves; refuse to accept things 'hook, line and sinker'. Effective leaders are able to study people to adequately understand verbal and non-verbal responses. In-fact, great leaders are "unshockable".

John 2:24-25 says, *"But Jesus did not commit himself unto them, because he knew all men, And needed not that any should testify of man: for he knew what was in man."*

The great Prophet Samuel would have made a big mistake in judgement and plunged Israel into a very disastrous end when he was to anoint a king from the household of Jesse in 1 Samuel 16:7, "*But the LORD said unto Samuel, Look not on his countenance, or on the height of his stature; because I have refused him: for the LORD seeth not as man seeth; for man looketh on the outward appearance, but the LORD looketh on the heart.*" Many leaders have fallen because they held people at face value.

We must however avoid the other extreme of becoming overly suspicious of people. Overlook many things, don't overdo anything, overcome all things but overall, be wise. Matthew 7:15-16 says, "*Beware of false prophets, which come to you in sheep's clothing, but inwardly they are ravening wolves. Ye shall know them by their fruits. Do men gather grapes of thorns, or figs of thistles?*"

2 Corinthians 11:13-14 says, "*For such are false apostles, deceitful workers, transforming themselves into the apostles of Christ. And no marvel; for Satan himself is transformed into an angel of light.*"

Every great leader will definitely face betrayal by their confidants. Many have fallen into big issues because they confided in the wrong people. Sometimes you will find out that those you have invested a lot in were running a different agenda all along and they will eventually abandon ship to set up their own establishment.

This is especially common in faith-based institutions and in politics, however this is unavoidable because we are all human. What will determine the effectiveness of one's leadership is how one handles these things.

Initially, I found it very difficult to handle such situations because I have always believed that the foundation of any good relationship is sincerity and honesty. So, I tended to blame people and generalize but I have come to realize that the statement of Paul was so apt when he said, *"They went out from us, but they were not of us; for if they had been of us, they would no doubt have continued with us: but they went out, that they might be made manifest that they were not all of us"* (1 John 2:19). John the Baptist also said *"A man can receive nothing, except it be given him from heaven"* (John 3:27).

Many great leaders of institutions have experienced people leaving them as Paul said *"At my first answer no man stood with me, but all men forsook me: I pray God that it may not be laid to their charge"* (2 Timothy 4:16). I know of a Pastor of one of the greatest ministries in America who said in the early part of his ministry, almost everyone left him and he had to stand alone with God to start from scratch. I also think about Jesus's experience when He spoke the truth to His apostles and *"From that time many of his disciples went back, and walked no more with him. Then said Jesus unto the twelve, Will ye also go away?"* (John 6: 66-67).

At such times, I have come to believe that God uses people to humble leaders, to define their mission appropriately, to help them trust in Him completely and to test their commitment to Him and to His mission.

In a sense, people deserting you or leaving the mission may be painful but if you persist with the mission, you will find out that it was for the best. God may have taken a decision to separate you because He knows people better than you do. I love the example of Joseph who said *"But as for you, you thought evil against me, but God meant it for good, to bring to pass, as it is this day, to save a great many people alive"* (Genesis 50:20).

On the flip side, when people leave you, it might be good to take time to engage them in order to find out areas of your leadership that occasioned such reaction and use the opportunity to make adjustments and reform your pattern of leadership. However, do not allow anyone's reaction or activity cause you to turn away from the mission that you have been called to.

eight

GIVING EXCUSES

It has been said that there are two kinds of leaders; those who give excuses and those who execute their duties. Great leaders never give excuses, they rise up to challenges. Leaders don't complain or find reasons why things will not work; they find a way to make things work.

Beware of excuses because they weaken your power to execute and consequently retard your progress. Excuses paralyze action, impede progress, destroy institutions and demean great people. When leaders give excuses, it shows that they are weak. Those who give excuses are good at nothing but excuses. Some even have *'Excusitis'* - inflammation of excuses. If giving excuses was to be monetized, many-a-mortal would be billionaires.

Proverbs 22:13 says, *"The slothful man saith, there is a lion without, I shall be slain in the streets.*

Excuses are not allowed in leadership and this was portrayed by Jesus when He selected those who would be His disciples in Luke 9:59-62 which says, *"And he said unto another, Follow me. But he said, Lord, suffer me first to go and bury my father. Jesus said unto him, Let the dead bury their dead: but go thou and preach the kingdom of God. And another also said, Lord, I will follow thee; but let me first go bid them farewell, which are at home at my house. And Jesus said unto him, No man, having put his hand to the plough, and looking back, is fit for the kingdom of God."*

If you want to be an effective leader, you must be responsible and relentless; go about every task with the spirit of excellence and don't give room for excuses. Do what is expected, fulfil your obligations, be functional, keep your promises, do what you ought to do and let your work speak. Go for it and turn your excuses to earnest pursuits. If you cannot find a way, gently bow out but please, stop giving excuses.

nine

REFUSING TO FIGHT BACK

Leaders must learn to be courageous when faced with pressure. They must not faint or quit in the face of adversity; they must talk back to the enemy. Leaders will be faced with various challenges, temptations, jealousies and many big problems but they must fight back. Never give in to pressure or glory in your weakness, fight back. Proverbs 24:10 says, *"If thou faint in the day of adversity, thy strength is small."*

In 1 Samuel 30:18-19, The families of David and his men families had been abducted by their enemies, David and his men pursued them, *"And David recovered all that the Amalekites had carried away: and David rescued his two wives. And there was nothing lacking to them, neither small nor great, neither sons nor daughters, neither spoil, nor any thing that they had taken to them: David recovered all."*

Strength qualifies you for a battle while courage keeps you fighting until victory is achieved. Joshua 1:9 says, *"Have I not commanded you? Be strong and of good courage; do not be afraid, nor be dismayed, for the Lord your God is with you wherever you go."*

Apostle Paul admonished us in Ephesians 6:10-13, *"Finally, my brethren, be strong in the Lord, and in the power of his might. Put on the whole armour of God, that ye may be able to stand against the wiles of the devil. For we wrestle not against flesh and blood, but against principalities, against powers, against the rulers of the darkness of this world, against spiritual wickedness in high places. Wherefore take unto you the whole armour of God, that ye may be able to withstand in the evil day, and having done all, to stand."*

The Bible further says in 2 Corinthians 10:4-5, *"For the weapons of our warfare are not carnal but mighty in God for pulling down strongholds, casting down arguments and every high thing that exalts itself against the knowledge of God, bringing every thought into captivity to the obedience of Christ."*

A great leader must however fight ethically and according to the principles of the Scripture. *"For God did not give us a spirit of timidity or cowardice or fear, but [He has given us a spirit] of power and of love and of sound judgment and personal discipline [abilities that result in a calm, well-balanced mind and self-control]"* (2 Timothy 1:7 AMP). 1 Timothy 6:12 also says, *"Fight the good fight of faith, lay hold on eternal life, to which you were also called and have confessed the good confession in the presence of many witnesses."*

James 4:7 says, *"Submit yourselves therefore to God. Resist the devil, and he will flee from you."* Therefore, as a leader, you must *"Be on your guard; stand firm in the faith; be courageous; be strong"* (1 Corinthians 16:13).

ten

FAINTING AND QUITTING

Great leaders don't just start projects, they take projects across the finishing line and finish well. If you quit, you will never come back to the same position and everything you have done will be trashed. Finishing is a sign of faithfulness; an example laid by God Himself. Finishing is it! The hallmark of greatness is seeing things to their end as Jesus said in Matthew 24:13, *"But he that shall endure unto the end, the same shall be saved."*

You cannot afford to be a quitter. Quitters are individuals who put a full stop where God has put a comma. Don't ever come to a point in life where you give up. Do not quit, for *"No man, having put his hand to the plough, and looking back, is fit for the kingdom of God"* (Luke 9:62).

Keep pursuing until you achieve the goal. When people throw stones at you, turn them to stepping stones. Leaders burn the bridges of the past but do not quit. They keep going on, striving and working hard. If you desire to succeed as a leader, you must *"not be weary in well doing: for in due season we shall reap, if we faint not* (Galatians 6:9).

Do not despise the little things or quit because things seem to be moving at a slow pace. It is commitment to little things that make you suitable for greater things; it is faithfulness to insignificant things that bring you to significance; it is doing the little things well that brings you recognition among great men. No matter what you have been called to do, just show up. When you make good use of your standing place, you will move the world.

1 Corinthians 15:58 says, *"Therefore, my beloved brethren, be ye steadfast, unmoveable, always abounding in the work of the Lord, forasmuch as ye know that your labour is not in vain in the Lord."*

Every leadership has an end which is not in the praises of men but in God's commendation as a good and faithful servant. Paul said in Philippians 3:14, *"I press toward the mark for the prize of the high calling of God in Christ Jesus."*

Keep pressing on and do not feel like a hero before you get to end of the journey. Be a finisher, flow with the power of

God and keep running the race until you reach the zenith. Philippians 1:6 says, *"Being confident of this very thing, that he which hath begun a good work in you will perform it until the day of Jesus Christ:"*

Acts 20:24 says, *"But none of these things move me, neither count I my life dear unto myself, so that I might finish my course with joy, and the ministry, which I have received of the Lord Jesus, to testify the gospel of the grace of God."*

A leader must be able to say, *"I have fought a good fight, I have finished my course, I have kept the faith: Henceforth there is laid up for me a crown of righteousness, which the Lord, the righteous judge, shall give me at that day: and not to me only, but unto all them also that love his appearing"* (1 Timothy 4:7-8).

God always reserves the crown till the end. Don't be scared of your obligations, get challenged by them and tap on divine strength.

eleven

REFUSING TO FLOW WITH THE POWER OF THE SPIRIT

Sometimes, people call the power of the spirit their gut feelings – a feeling they have within them that they cannot explain. I consider this to be the flow of the Spirit. It was said of Jesus Christ that *"He was led of the Spirit"* (Matthew 4:1). Paul said in Romans 9:1, *"I say the truth in Christ, I lie not, my conscience also bearing me witness in the Holy Ghost."* The spirit is an inner witness, inner helper and inner guide.

Essentially, leadership is flowing in tandem with the power of God, either in the secular or the sacred calling but more so in sacred callings. God must be the Captain of the boat. Romans 8:14 says, *"For as many as are led by the Spirit of God, these are sons of God."*

Every leader must seek the Spirit consistently for guidance, inspiration, invigoration and recalibration of the calling. The leader must be continually under the influence of the Holy Spirit. Zechariah 4:6 says, *"So he answered and said to me: "This is the word of the Lord to Zerubbabel: 'Not by might nor by power, but by My Spirit,' Says the Lord of hosts."* The Scriptures say in Ephesians 5:18, *"And do not be drunk with wine, in which is dissipation; but be filled with the Spirit."*

Everything we find in the Bible has been as a result of the power of the Spirit of God moving in the lives of men. The Spirit is the medium of transmission of God's power.

A great leader must study times and seasons and be sensitive to instructions from the Holy Spirit per time. 1 Corinthians 2:10 says, *"But God hath revealed them unto us by his Spirit: for the Spirit searcheth all things, yea, the deep things of God."*

Being rigid and sticking to the status quo leads to disaster. The Lord does not show us the full picture all at once, so a leader must always flow with the Spirit of God to receive instructions as they are revealed. 1 Corinthians 13:9 says, *"For we know in part, and we prophesy in part."*

Never quench the Spirit in your quest for worldly fame. It is the Holy Spirit that will sustain you when the challenges come. Do not walk ahead of God, do not walk against God; make sure you are walking with God. John 14:26 says, *"But the Comforter, which is the Holy Ghost, whom the Father will send in my name, he shall teach you all things, and bring all things to your remembrance, whatsoever I have said unto you."* Isaiah 30:21 says, *"And thine ears shall hear a word behind thee, saying, This is the way, walk ye in it, when ye turn to the right hand, and when ye turn to the left."* The wise Solomon said in Proverbs 3:5-6, *"Trust in the LORD with all thine heart; and lean not unto thine own understanding. In all thy ways acknowledge him, and he shall direct thy paths."*

Our Lord Jesus Christ acknowledged His dependence on God in John 5:19, *"Then answered Jesus and said unto them, Verily, verily, I say unto you, The Son can do nothing of himself, but what he seeth the Father do: for what things soever he doeth, these also doeth the Son likewise."* In John 15:5 He said, *"I am the vine, ye are the branches: He that abideth in me, and I in him, the same bringeth forth much fruit: for without me ye can do nothing."*

twelve

NOT KNOWING WHEN TO TRANSIT

Leadership is often divided into phases. Leaders step into leadership positions, deliver their best and exit to other areas of calling. History is rife with stories of sit-tight leaders who refuse to transition or move on thereby destroying their reputation and the institution they seek to build. Every leader should know when to leave the stage and get involved in other things. By doing so, they make room for other leaders, for younger minds with brighter and more innovative ideas. Transition can also take place when you find that you are no longer effective or useful to the institution. I started out my leadership ministry by reaching out translocally and internationally. After some years, I started a local church and from there created an online presence where I have been able to reach a larger audience with my messages on leadership and ministry.

This has given me an experience, a new perspective, improved my creative output and rejuvenated my energy.

Effective leaders move when the ovation is loudest and not when they become a problem. No matter how good a leader is, his leadership is not deemed great until he achieves a successful transitioning. There is a Latin phrase recited every time a new Pope is coronated, it is, "Sic transit gloria mundi". This means "So perishes the glory of the world". Every position of leadership has an expiration date and we have to prepare for a transitioning in order to have a greater relevance in our generation and in the generations to come.

Many leaders often face the temptation to keep holding on to the position and this is sometimes out of fear of losing control or just out of love for the routine. Great leaders must consider what might happen if they are taken out of the picture or get too old to be effective. The future of every institution is too big for the ego of one person who does not know when to quit, hand over to someone else and move on. Philippians 2:2-3 says, *"Let nothing be done through strife or vainglory; but in lowliness of mind let each esteem other better than themselves. Look not every man on his own things, but every man also on the things of others."*

Overstaying in a leadership position often leads to complacency and stagnancy which will impede the growth of the institution. As Jesus said in John 16:7, *"Nevertheless I tell you the truth; It is expedient for you that I go away: for if I go not away, the Comforter will not come unto you; but if I depart, I will send him unto you."*

How then does a leader prepare for transitioning? A leader mentors a generation and seeks people to mentor and bring up from time to time. They not only do great works but train people who will take their place after they have left the position. Jesus prepared His disciples way ahead of His death by empowering them for the work He came to earth for. We read in Matthew 10:1, *"And when he had called unto him his twelve disciples, he gave them power against unclean spirits, to cast them out, and to heal all manner of sickness and all manner of disease."* David also prepared his son Solomon with instructions on how to carry on after him and how to walk in the way of kings. 2 Chronicles 28:11-12 says, *"Then David gave to Solomon his son the pattern of the porch, and of the houses thereof, and of the treasuries thereof, and of the upper chambers thereof, and of the inner parlours thereof, and of the place of the mercy seat, And the pattern of all that he had by the spirit, of the courts of the house of the LORD, and of all the chambers round about, of the treasuries of the house of God, and of the treasuries of the dedicated things".*

Leaders must avoid portraying themselves as invincible, indispensable or irreplaceable. This has been one of the greatest pitfalls of great leaders all through civilization. Many leaders throughout history were loved and respected by the people but refused to hand over power when they were due to do so. Thus they became dictatorial, fell out of favour with their followers and lost their reputation with the people who had once held them in high esteem. Another danger of staying in a position for too long is the risk of overfamiliarity with the people which will eventually breed contempt.

Effective leaders learn to mix their circle of influence between leaders who are mature and those who are upcoming. They must make way for the younger ones to manifest and lead while they observe, thus allowing them to have a feel of leadership. The Lord instructed Moses to transfer leadership to Joshua in Numbers 27:18-21, *"So the Lord said to Moses, "Take Joshua son of Nun, a man in whom is the spirit, and lay your hand on him. Have him stand before Eleazar the priest and the entire assembly and commission him in their presence. Give him some of your authority so the whole Israelite community will obey him. He is to stand before Eleazar the priest, who will obtain decisions for him by inquiring of the Urim before the Lord. At his command he and the entire community of the Israelites will go out, and at his command they will come in."*

The effective leader should also be open to the upcoming generation for new ideas; though they may tend to be idealistic, the leader's openness to their ideas will not make the leader anachronistic.

Leadership transitioning allows the leaders see other things they can do and other aspects where they can be impactful as they move from one level of leadership to another. As the leader gets older, more emphasis should be placed on mentorship and developing others rather than the physical activities involved in leadership. Paul exemplified this when he said to Timothy in 2 Timothy 2:2, *"And the things that thou hast heard of me among many witnesses, the same commit thou to faithful men, who shall be able to teach others also."*

As a leader, stepping down from a position of active leadership will give one the time to recreate, regain health, write books and probably get involved in online networking which are less stressful. The leader is afforded more time to balance other aspects of life which may have been neglected during the period of active leadership. It also gives the leaders the opportunity to look back on their leadership styles and spot the missing gaps which should not be passed on to the next generation.

AFTERTHOUGHTS

Leadership has always been a very fascinating topic for me and I have learnt from my personal experience and the numerous books I have read that leadership is a journey and not a destination. It is important for you to realize that learning in leadership is an ongoing process that continues all through life.

As we meet with new experiences and challenges, our perspective of leadership will change. The requirements of leadership change depending on the positions we hold, the occupations we are involved in and sometimes the culture and environment we live in.

However, the core principles of leadership hardly change, which are service and sacrifice as exemplified by the greatest model of leadership – Jesus Christ.

Always remember that leadership is never about the leader but about the people; it is bringing positive influence to our world and taking the people to a place of fulfilment in life.

I sincerely appreciate you for buying and reading this book on Effective Leadership and I look forward to discussions with you on the topic. You can send me an email at gregerhabor7@yahoo.com with your questions, comments and feedbacks and I would be glad to respond.

You can also connect with me via online platforms where I post inspirational messages daily:

Website - gregerhabor.com

Telegram - Rev. Prof. Greg. Erhabor

Podcast - Greg Erhabor Hope Podcast

Facebook, Instagram and Twitter - @gregerhabor

I encourage you to get copies of other books I have written which are available on Amazon, Kindle and at the Spokesman Resource Center in Ile Ife.

NOTES

1. Drucker, P.F. (2006). *The effective executive.* HarperCollins.
2. Goleman, D., Boyatzis, R. E., & McKee, A. (2013). *Primal leadership: Unleashing the power of emotional intelligence.* Harvard Business Press.
3. Covey, S.R. (2013). *The 7 Habits of highly effective people.* USA: RosettaBooks LLC, Electronic Edition.
4. Collins, J. (2011). *Good to Great.* New York, USA: HarperCollins Publisher.
5. Erhabor G. (2017). *1001 Timeless Inspirational Quotes.* Nigeria: Spokesman Books/Signet Impressions. Amazon-Kindle. https://amzn.to3Egolso
6. Erhabor G. (2021). *iHope Spokesman Inspirational Nuggets.* Nigeria: Spokesman Books/Signet Academic Publications.
7. Covey, S. R., & Merrill, A. R. (1993). *First things first.* New York: Simon & Schuster.

8. Goodridge A. *Time to focus on you using the 4 pillars of self-leadership*. adflorem.com.
9. Duckworth A.L., Peterson C, Matthews M.D., Kelly D.R. *Grit: Perseverance and Passion for Long-Term Goals.* J Pers Soc Psychol. 2007 Jun;92(6): 1087-101. doi: 10.1037/0022-3514.92.6.1087.
10. Csikszentmihalyi, Mihaly (1990). *Flow: The Psychology of Optimal Experience*. New York: Harper and Row. ISBN 0-06-092043-2
11. Gaines Jeffrey. (2020 Nov 17). *The Philosophy of Ikigai: 3 Examples About Finding Purpose.* PositivePsychology.com. retrieved from https://positivepsychology.com/ikigai/
12. Sinek, S. (2011). *Start with why.* Penguin Books.
13. Kouzes, J. M., & Posner, B. Z. (2017). *The leadership challenge* (6th ed.). John Wiley & Sons.
14. Dhiman, Satinder. (2011). *Walking the Talk: A Story about Mahatma Gandhi.* 10.1057/9780230370432_68.
15. Tuckman, B. W., & Jensen, M. A. C. (1977). *Stages of small-group development revisited*. Group & organization studies, 2(4), 419-427.
16. Loiuse Emma (2022 May 19). shttps://www.thecoachingtools company.com/wheel-of-life-complete-guide-everything-you-need-to-know/

ABOUT THE AUTHOR

Gregory Erhabor is a leadership enthusiast, a life coach and a conference speaker. He has been a consultant chest physician for over three decades and also a professor of medicine for over twenty years. He trained in Nigeria and the Great Britain. Greg has authored several books on different subjects including leadership, Christian faith and medicine. He loves God and he is committed to the service of humanity. He is a pastor and also the founder of Asthma and Chest Care Foundation, a nonprofit organization that supports asthmatics in Nigeria and elsewhere. Gregory is married to Ayodele and they have three children.

The One-Life Books
by Gregory Erhabor

Ten Principles for Deep-rooted Success and Fulfilment in Life

In this book you will find a careful assemblage of universally relevant and proven principles for indelible impact. The book offers essential tenets that can set you off for an effective, meaningful and impactful life. There are hands-on illustrations of how to achieve this. The book will take you through a journey in search of that 'one thing' that defines you as an individual. Don't just flip through the pages; savour everything therein.

11 Principles for Maximizing your Life and Time

In the eleventh hour that we are in today, managing your life and time is very crucial. This book will equip you with eleven fundamental principles that can steer you in the right direction of your life. It is suitable for everyone and my hope is that it will help you (re)focus your life in a way that will help you maximize your time. As you imbibe these principles and apply them, I expect that there will be dramatic turnaround in your life.

Other Books by the Author

- 100 Ornaments of Wisdom for Exceptional Living
- Loyalty: The Path to Greatness
- The Making of a Great Pastor
- 12 Principles for All-round
- Success and Eternal Significance
- Balancing Life And Work in the 21st Century
- Your Time in Your Hand
- Principles of Academic Excellence
- From Worry to Well-being
- Seize Your Day: Control your Destiny
- The Power of Joy
- The Seven Most Effective Affirmations
- Towards Achieving your Goals
- Seeds of Excellence
- Dare to Fulfill yyour Destiny
- God Centered Prosperity
- Making your Life Count
- 101 Quotable Quotes on Prayer- Apples of Gold
- The Test, Travails and Triumph Of Leadership
- It Pays to Forgive